THE

TRANSCONTINENTAL
RAILROAD

by
LINDA THOMPSON

Rourke
Publishing LLC
Vero Beach, Florida 32964

www.rourkepublishing.com

PHOTO CREDITS:
Courtesy Bancroft Library: page 13; Courtesy California State Railroad Museum Foundation: page 19; Dellenbaugh, Frederick S., *Breaking the Wilderness*, 1905: pages 26, 30, 34; Courtesy Library of Congress, Prints and Photographs Division: Title page, pages 10, 14, 25, 27, 32, 42; Courtesy Library of Congress, Rare Book and Special Collections Division: pages 8, 16, 41; Courtesy NASA: page 7; Courtesy National Archives and Records Administration: Cover, pages 11, 36; Courtesy National Parks Service: page 36 Courtesy Scotts Bluff National Monument: pages 21, 26, 28-29, 31, 38; Courtesy Union Pacific Railroad: page 15.

SPECIAL NOTE: Further information about people's names shown in the text in bold can be found on page 43. More information about glossary terms in bold in the text can be found on pages 46 and 47.

DESIGN: ROHM PADILLA
LAYOUT/PRODUCTION: ELIZABETH BENDER

Library of Congress Cataloging-in-Publication Data

Thompson, Linda, 1941-
    The Transcontinental Railroad / Linda Thompson.
        p. cm. -- (Expansion of America)
    Includes bibliographical references and index.
    ISBN 1-59515-227-X (hardcover)
    1. Pacific railroads--Juvenile literature. I. Title. II. Series:
Thompson, Linda, 1941-   Expansion of America.
    TF25.P2T48 2004
    385'.0978--dc22

                2004010035

TITLE PAGE IMAGE
Transcontinental Railroad at Giant Bluff in South Dakota

TABLE OF CONTENTS

Horatio Allen

Only 20 years after it became independent, the United States gained a region that doubled the country's size. And barely 50 years later, it reached across immense plains and towering mountain ranges to touch the Pacific Ocean. How it grew so fast in such a short time is still an amazing tale. One key to this rapid growth was the building of railroads.

When the 19th century began, the United States had only 17 states and one large **territory**. The country's western border was the Mississippi River. But by the end of 1803, President **Thomas Jefferson** had bought the vast and unknown land called Louisiana from France. Stretching from the Mississippi River to the Rocky Mountains, it included 828,000 square miles (2,144,510 square km) of unknown land. This land was now available for exploration and settlement.

Before the railroad was built, explorers and traders headed west in carts pulled by livestock.

4

At first a few explorers, traders, and trappers set out on foot and horseback, seeking ways to cross the wide rivers, steep mountain ranges, and blistering hot deserts of the West. In the 1840s, families began to head west in covered wagons drawn by mules or oxen. The journey by wagon took four months or more. By the 1850s, stagecoaches pulled by fast horses began to carry mail and passengers from the Missouri River to the West Coast in less than three weeks. But nothing could carry heavy loads, such as timber, coal, iron, steel, livestock, or equipment better than a line of cars pulled by a steam engine over steel rails.

The first American railroad was a small horse-drawn line in Massachusetts that opened in 1826. A year before, **John Stevens** had built a steam locomotive in New Jersey, but the public saw it as a toy. In 1829, an engineer named **Horatio Allen** brought one of the new "**Iron Horses**" from England and tested it on a 3-mile (4.8-km) section of track at a Pennsylvania coal mine. Within a few years, "railroad fever" had swept the country. By 1840, the East had nearly 3,000 miles (4,800 km) of track, more than the total in European countries combined. In February 1854, the first train from the East reached the Mississippi River. And 10 years later, there were 33,860 miles (54,200 km) of completed railway in the United States, with 16,000 more miles (25,745 km) under construction.

PUFFING BILLY

From England came reports of steam-propelled engines that were replacing horses. An engine called "Puffing Billy," announced in 1813, could haul 10 coal wagons at 5 miles (8 km) an hour. And in 1829, "The Rocket" was invented—the first true "Iron Horse." It traveled an amazing 29 miles (47 km) an hour.

A steam-powered engine

As early as 1830, politicians and others had talked about ways to build a **transcontinental** railroad, linking the Atlantic and Pacific coasts. But many problems had to be solved first. An important question was how to pay for such an immense project. Just getting supplies, including tons of timber and steel, to the point of construction— the forward end of the rails— would be very expensive.

Much of the land a railroad would cross had few people except for **nomadic** groups of Native Americans, who followed the buffalo. They could be expected to strongly resist any railroad across their lands. They knew what it could bring— thousands of people and the eventual loss of their way of life and their land. It would cost millions of dollars to find good workers to build the railroad, feed them during the 6 to 10 years the project was expected to take and also protect them and the railroad from attacks by angry Natives.

To build a railroad to the West Coast, construction crews would have to cross high mountains, thick forests, burning deserts, and deep canyons. The most dreaded obstacle was the **Sierra Nevada**, a mountain range that divides California from the rest of the country. A massive block of granite, it rises from 4,000 feet to 7,000 feet (1,200 to 2,135 m) with 12 peaks higher than 14,000 feet (4,270 m). The mountain **summits** were covered with ice much of the year, and snow drifted as deep as 60 feet (18 m) in winter. Explorers and pioneers had frozen to death trying to cross those mountains.

Aerial view of the southern Sierra Nevada Mountains

The debate was interrupted by the Civil War, which divided North and South over the issue of slavery. The war exploded across the country from 1861 to 1865, taking 618,000 lives, ruining the South, and destroying relations between North and South. Still, in spite of the war, Congress managed to approve a transcontinental railroad, select a route, and build much of it. When the last spike was driven on

Government report about the impracticalities of building a railroad

May 10, 1869, national feelings of pride and triumph helped ease the bitterness and sadness left in the war's wake.

In 1867 the United States had purchased Alaska from Russia for $7,200,000. Although Alaska would not be settled for some time, the rest of the empty **frontier** soon vanished. During the 1880s, more than 40,000 miles (64,360 km) of railroad track were laid west of the Mississippi River. By 1900 the United States had 14 times as many people as in 1803, and 25 percent of them lived in the West. **Historians** say that the American people's greatest achievement in the 19th century was ending slavery. But the next greatest achievement was building the transcontinental railroad, which let the country complete its westward growth and emerge as the strongest economic power in the world.

Chapter II: VISIONS OF SPEED AND MONEY

After gold was discovered in California in 1848, followed by smaller gold and silver rushes in Nevada and Colorado, building a railroad seemed ever more urgent. It took months of land or sea travel just to get minerals and other goods to market and to bring supplies to miners and settlers. To tap the rich resources of the West, people were convinced, everything would have to move much faster.

One of the early supporters of a transcontinental railroad was **Asa Whitney**, a New England merchant who wanted to trade with China. In 1845, he asked Congress to authorize a survey for a route between the 42nd and

Asa Whitney

45th **parallels**. He offered to build the railroad himself if Congress would give him a strip of land 60 miles (96.5 km) wide, reaching from Lake Michigan to the Pacific Ocean. Few at the time took him seriously.

Stephen A. Douglas

But Americans knew that someday a railroad would be built. And when it happened, whatever route it followed across the country would bring prosperity to that region. Towns and farms would appear along the tracks. Settlers would follow the railroad because they would be able to depend on receiving supplies and sending their farm produce to market.

Cities began competing to become the railroad's eastern **terminus** by holding railroad **conventions**. Senator **Stephen A. Douglas** of Illinois wanted the eastern end-point to be Chicago. Southern Senators, such as Thomas Hart Benton of Missouri and Sam Houston of Texas, insisted on a southern route. Major conventions were held in St. Louis, Missouri; Memphis, Tennessee; and other cities, but the only thing people could agree upon was the need for a survey. On March 1, 1853, Congress authorized the **Corps of Topographical Engineers** to find "the most practical and economic route for a railroad from the Mississippi River to the Pacific Ocean."

The survey's findings, published in 1855, showed that four routes were practical. Senator Douglas proposed that the federal government build three railroad lines—a Northern Pacific line from Wisconsin to Puget Sound, Washington; a Central Pacific from Missouri or Iowa to San Francisco; and a Southern Pacific from Texas to Southern California.

It was going to be difficult to pay for even one railroad, and Congress concluded that private **capitalists** would demand rewards for investing so much money. In the past, Congress had given public lands to states, and the states had issued **bonds** to sell to investors, using the money to build railroads. A new way of funding this enormous project was needed. It would involve lending money directly to the railroad companies and giving them large amounts of land on either side of the tracks. The companies could sell the land to help pay for construction.

View from the summit looking west along the 49th Parallel by James Alden, official artist of the U.S. survey team, 1859-60

11

In the midst of this planning, tensions between North and South were building to intolerable levels. In 1861, 11 southern states **seceded** from the union, triggering the Civil War. With no southern politicians left to argue for a railroad route through the South, Congress selected a central route. Now, someone needed to step forward and create the Central Pacific Railroad.

Theodore Judah, a civil engineer from Connecticut, was that person. He had gone to California to help build a short rail line from Sacramento to the gold fields east of town. He was so eager to build a transcontinental railroad that he could hardly speak of anything else. People who doubted that such a railroad could be built called him "Crazy Judah." After several trips to **lobby** Congressmen in Washington, D.C., Judah decided to find the best pass across the Sierra Nevada. In 1860, he explored the mountains and concluded that **Donner Summit** was the best crossing point.

Judah interested four businessmen in Sacramento in his ideas. **Charles Crocker** owned a clothing store, **Collis Huntington** and **Mark Hopkins** were partners in a hardware store, and **Leland Stanford** had a grocery business. These men were active in the new **Republican** party of **Abraham Lincoln**, who had just been elected president of the country. Lincoln strongly supported a Pacific railroad. Crocker was a state representative, and Stanford would become California's governor the following year. Later, when their business skills and political connections had made them some of the most powerful men in the country, these men would be known as the "Big Four."

(Top) Mark Hopkins, Collis P. Huntington, (center) Theodore Judah, (bottom) Leland Stanford and Charles Crocker

On June 28, 1861, with the Civil War underway, Judah and his partners **incorporated** the Central Pacific Railroad of California. Stanford was president and Judah chief engineer. They had a total of $159,000 in **assets.** But estimates showed it was going to cost $12,500,000 just to cross the Sierra Nevada Mountains!

The Big Four sent Judah to Washington, D.C., with Central Pacific stock to offer lawmakers. He presented the results of his surveys and lobbied tirelessly for the railroad. While he was there, Congress passed and President Lincoln signed a bill authorizing a transcontinental railroad. On July 1, 1862, Judah wired Leland Stanford that his mission had been successful.

General Grenville Dodge

DODGE AND LINCOLN

General **Grenville Dodge** was a Civil War hero who became chief engineer for the Union Pacific in 1866. In 1859, he had met Abraham Lincoln, a railroad lawyer running for President. Lincoln's first words to Dodge were, "What's the best route for a Pacific railroad to the West?" Dodge convinced him to build the transcontinental railroad in the Platte River valley and later got him to support bills that funded the railroad.

Meanwhile, in the East, **Thomas Durant** was a railroad promoter and **financier**. He was known for his dishonest dealings, which enriched him but often left others poorer. He boasted that his only interest in railroad building was the money to be made.

Durant formed a railroad company called the Union Pacific, and Congress chose it to build the eastern end of the transcontinental line. The Central Pacific would begin in Sacramento and climb the Sierra Nevada. The Union Pacific would begin at Omaha, Nebraska, cross the Rocky Mountains over South Pass, and meet the California Pacific at the California-Nevada state line.

Union Pacific Railroad logos from 1863 (top) and today (bottom)

15

WHAT THEY RECEIVED

Federal loans to the two companies in the form of 30-year bonds eventually totaled $96 million. The bonds paid six percent interest a year. The Union Pacific received 19.1 million acres (7,735,500 hectares) of land and the Central Pacific about 7.3 million acres (2,956,500 hectares). Both companies made millions of dollars by selling stock and bonds.

Union Pacific Railroad Company report, *Progress of Their Road*

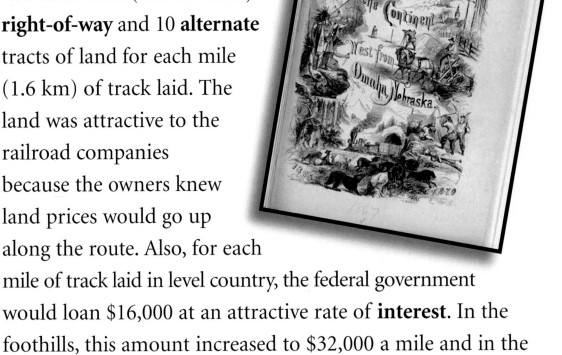

Congress gave each railroad a 400-foot-wide (122-m-wide) **right-of-way** and 10 **alternate** tracts of land for each mile (1.6 km) of track laid. The land was attractive to the railroad companies because the owners knew land prices would go up along the route. Also, for each mile of track laid in level country, the federal government would loan $16,000 at an attractive rate of **interest**. In the foothills, this amount increased to $32,000 a mile and in the mountains to $48,000 a mile.

DEATH OF JUDAH

On January 8, 1863, while the first spikes were being driven for the Central Pacific Railroad, Theodore Judah was dying in New York. His relationship with his partners had been turning sour, and he had gone east to seek money to try to buy out the Big Four. Crossing Panama, he had caught **yellow fever**. Judah died on November 2, 1863.

The Central Pacific began the following year, but the Union Pacific took two more years to get started. One reason the Central Pacific was more prepared was its close connections with the state of California. The Big Four got the state to lend them an additional $1,659,000 for construction. Also, Stanford and the others loaned about $60,000 of their own money.

Railroad companies were paid $48,000 per mile to lay track through mountain terrain like the Sierra Nevadas (below).

On January 8, 1863, in Sacramento, Charles Crocker supervised the placing of the first rails of the transcontinental railroad. The directors of the Central Pacific held a **ground-breaking** ceremony. Meanwhile, a locomotive they had ordered from the East arrived from its voyage around South America. When it was unloaded at the Sacramento dock, it fell into the river. Crocker and Hopkins, who headed the construction crews, hauled it out, named it "Governor Stanford" after their partner who had been elected California's governor, and sent the locomotive to where the first rails were being laid.

Typical steam locomotive

LOCOMOTIVES

The Central Pacific paid $79,752 for two locomotives in the beginning. They were necessary to travel on the rails as they were built, pulling cars that carried materials, supplies, and men to the construction camps. They provided sleeping and dining quarters. Also, the companies were able to earn money from freight charges on sections of track completed. In 1865, the Central Pacific earned $280,000 on freight charges.

"Governor Stanford" in the California State Railroad Museum

In the East, the Union Pacific held a grand groundbreaking ceremony on December 1, 1863, in Omaha—but no track was actually built until the middle of 1865. Durant was too busy setting up ways in which he could sell **shares** of his railroad and make money before the first rails were laid. He also distributed shares of the company among politicians to make sure they would vote for bills that would favor his activities.

HOW RAILROAD OWNERS GOT RICH

Both railroads set up privately held construction companies so the owners could award themselves inflated contracts for laying track. For example, the Central Pacific gave its construction arm, the Contract and Finance Company, contracts equal to $90,000,000. But the cost of the work—paid for by grants and loans from the government—was only $32,200,000. The Big Four pocketed the difference. The name "Crédit Mobilier," the Union Pacific's construction branch, became a synonym for corruption after its owners transferred federal money to themselves before and during construction.

The Central Pacific made slow progress. Only 20 miles (32 km) of rail were laid down in 1864, 20 miles (32 km) in 1865, 30 miles (48 km) in 1866, and 46 miles (74 km) in 1867. The war, which ended in 1865, had caused a shortage of materials. Steel rails jumped from $55 a ton (.91 metric ton) in 1861 to $115 in 1863. Railroad building was unbelievably expensive—the 20 miles of track built in 1865 cost $6 million! Realizing that both railroads were struggling for money, Congress passed a law that made railroad investing more attractive. Railroads were given twice as much land (20 tracts per mile) and more shares were issued. At last, investors began buying railroad stocks and bonds.

Chapter III: ACHIEVING THE IMPOSSIBLE

Charles Crocker supervised construction for the Central Pacific. At first, he hired Irish immigrants and anyone else who applied for the backbreaking work. The men used picks, shovels, carts, and wheelbarrows to remove immense amounts of dirt and rock. When the **grade** was even and ties were in place, the rail crews laid steel rails exactly 4 feet 8-1/2 inches (1.44 m) apart, then spiked them in with blows from a **sledgehammer**—three blows to each spike. For this work, the men earned three dollars a day plus meals.

A work crew laying track

Stanford's geologists claimed that the base of the Sierra Nevada Mountains started in the Sacramento Valley, a good 24 miles (38 km) west of where the mountains actually began. Others disagreed, so Stanford suggested letting President Lincoln decide. Busier than ever with the Civil War, Lincoln consented to the geologists' claim. This meant that the Central Pacific could collect $48,000 a mile well before it reached the mountains.

The workers were more interested in mining than in laying track, so once they reached the foothills many ran off to the Nevada mines. In 1864, 1,900 out of 2,000 men hired left for the mines. So in 1865, Crocker suggested to **James Strobridge**, his construction superintendent, that they try Chinese laborers. More than 25,000 Chinese had arrived in northern California since the beginning of the Gold Rush. Strobridge resisted, but Crocker pointed out that Chinese would work for only $25 a month, less than half of what the Irish demanded, and they would supply their own food. "Did they not build the Chinese wall—the biggest piece of masonry in the world?" Crocker asked.

Chinese workers hammering railroad spikes

Strobridge agreed to try 50 Chinese, and if they worked well he would hire more. Within a few weeks Crocker had agents in every California town signing up Chinese men. Strobridge boasted that they were the best workers in the world. By the end of 1865, every available Chinese man in the state was working on the railroad, and Leland Stanford was attempting to bring more from China.

The Central Pacific struggled slowly up the slopes of the Sierra Nevada. In the Sierra, snowdrifts as deep as 60 feet (18.3 m) were common, settling into ice walls as hard as iron in the spring. Using pickaxes and powder, the Chinese inched their way through these frozen walls. After the harsh winter of 1867, the Central Pacific built wooden snow sheds to keep the snow from covering the tracks.

The Chinese, who were experts at building in rock, volunteered to blast in a place called "Cape Horn," the steep-walled canyon of the American River's North Fork. The workers asked that reeds from San Francisco marshes be brought to the construction site. At night, they wove round, waist-high reed baskets similar to baskets their ancestors had used in China. Hanging in these baskets alongside the canyon's rock face, they drilled holes, tamped in **black powder**, set fuses, and hollered for the crews above to pull them away as the powder exploded.

Near the summit of the Sierra Nevada, thousands of Chinese dug and blasted their way through the mountains. Eight thousand men worked in three shifts, night and day, building 12 tunnels from 800 to 1,650 feet (244 to 503 m) in length at altitudes above 6,000 feet (1,830 m) in temperatures below freezing.

Back east, after finally beginning construction in June 1865, the Union Pacific had a slow start. By the end of the year, it had laid only 40 miles (64 km) of track from Omaha. But after the war ended, hundreds of Irish laborers came searching for work. By late 1866 the Union Pacific was installing at least a mile (1.6 km) of track a day.

NITROGLYCERIN

Black powder could be used to break granite, but **nitroglycerin** was quicker and more effective. However, it is a highly unstable compound. When a dockhand in Panama dropped a crate of it that was bound for California, he blew himself and dozens of other workers to pieces. A similar explosion blew up the Wells Fargo freight office in San Francisco. But because it speeded up the work so much, Strobridge used it in the Sierra Nevada, especially in the **Summit Tunnel**. Using "nitro," workers were able to build two feet (0.61 m) of tunnel a day.

A black cloud from an explosive blast on the side of a mountain

TRESTLE CONSTRUCTION

In 1865 the California engineers decided to build wooden
trestles because it was impossible to bridge the gaps
that the train had to cross with earthen embankments. The
trestles were supported on the trunks of enormous trees set
into masonry. The crews cut giant firs, pines, and redwood
trees and shipped them to Sacramento sawmills where
they were made into lumber and sent back. Then the crews
built trestles as high as 100 feet (30.5 m), which resembled
giant, many-legged insects. Though they looked rickety,
the trestles were strong enough to support a train with
many cars.

Two examples of trestle construction

In early 1866, Durant put two brothers in charge of Union Pacific construction. **Dan Casement** managed **logistics**, while **John ("Jack") Casement** supervised the crews. When Grenville Dodge left the Army and joined the company in May 1866, the construction camps began operating like a military unit. The "advance guard" of surveyors went into the countryside, followed by graders. This crew cut through the gorges, graded the roadbed, and built bridges. Then came the "main army" to place the ties, lay track, spike down the rails, adjust the alignment, and get the road ready for use. Behind them rolled the construction train cars. One car carried tools, one was a blacksmith shop, another had dining tables and a kitchen. Others had bunk beds, and several **flatcars** carried road-building materials.

Railroad engineers with surveyors' tools and measuring sticks in the late 1800s

The Union Pacific crew worked with a rhythm—4 rails placed a minute, 3 strokes to a spike, 10 spikes to a rail, 400 rails to a mile. Every 30 seconds, the track boss shouted "Down!" signaling the men to drop the rails into place. The Irish crews sang in time, making up songs such as "Whoops Along, Luiza Jane," "Pat Maloy," and "I'm a Rambling Rake of Poverty, the Son of a Gambolier."

The Casement brothers paid each man three dollars a day if the crew laid at least a mile and a half of rail. When they could lay two miles (3.2 km) a day, the pay went up to four dollars. But in the summer of 1866, news arrived that gave them a **motive** for working even faster. Congress had decided that the Central Pacific should lay track into Nevada and beyond until the two lines came together. Now, the race began in earnest because all government **subsidies**, loans, land grants, and fares that were attached to each mile of rail would go to the company responsible for building that mile.

In the summer of 1867, the Central Pacific crossed the summit of the Sierras. By the end of that year, the Union Pacific had passed Cheyenne, Wyoming. Grenville Dodge, in charge of choosing the route, drove it over the Laramie Hills and across Wyoming to the top of the Rocky Mountains. Thomas Durant telegraphed Stanford in the West: "We send you greeting from the highest summit our line crosses between the Atlantic and the Pacific Oceans, 8,200 feet [2,500 m] above tidewater." Stanford replied: "Though you may approach the union of the two roads faster than ourselves you cannot exceed us in earnestness of desire for that great event. We cheerfully yield you the palm of superior elevation; 7,042 feet [2,146 m] has been quite sufficient to satisfy our highest ambition. May your descent be easy and rapid."

"Westward America" is a mural that depicts the evolution of transportation on the plains, from Indian travois to modern airplanes.

General **William Sherman**, who had led Union forces in the Civil War, was responsible for keeping peace with the Sioux, Cheyenne, and other Plains tribes. When Durant gave him a ride on the first 16 miles (25.7 km) of rail, Sherman had remarked, "This is a great enterprise but I hardly expect to live to see it completed."

As the railroad crossed the Plains, Native Americans realized that it posed the greatest threat to their way of life that had yet come along. Unlike emigrants, who passed through their lands, the people brought by the railroad stayed and built towns. This invasion would destroy the buffalo and with it the entire Plains culture. So the Sioux, Cheyenne, Arapaho, and others struck back.

General William Sherman in council with members of the Sioux

Pawnee in front of a large earth lodge

The Sioux and Cheyenne attacked construction crews several times during 1867. They pulled up some track, derailing a locomotive and killing its engineer and **brakeman**. Sherman sent four companies of **Pawnee**, who were enemies of the Sioux and Cheyenne, to guard construction crews. But the Southern Cheyenne wrecked another Union Pacific freight train at Plum Creek, Nebraska, killing the crew, while the Sioux attacked surveyors in Wyoming. Sherman called a meeting with the tribes at Fort Laramie in September 1867. The chiefs tried to explain that the railroad was destroying their way of life, and game was already getting scarce. Sherman replied that they must accept the lands designated for them. "We will build iron roads, and you cannot stop the locomotives any more than you can stop the sun or the moon," he said.

By 1868, the Sioux had been persuaded to sign treaties that moved them to South Dakota, with eastern Wyoming as their hunting ground. The Crow were confined to a section of central Montana, and the other Plains tribes went to reservations in Oklahoma. Although there would still be battles ahead, the day of free-roaming Native Americans had ended.

Chapter IV: THE JOINING OF THE TRACKS

In November 1868 Stanford met with Thomas Durant to decide where the railroads would join. Each man stubbornly believed his crew could lay rail faster than the other, and they refused to decide.

As the two companies raced toward each other, they began building less carefully. In their haste, the bosses told themselves that everything could be fixed later. But a few years after the railroad's completion, the American people were shocked to learn that hundreds of miles of the new railroad had to be replaced, using taxpayers' money. Poorly built rail joints, embankments, and trestles were collapsing. Sharp curves had to be straightened and rough grades reworked.

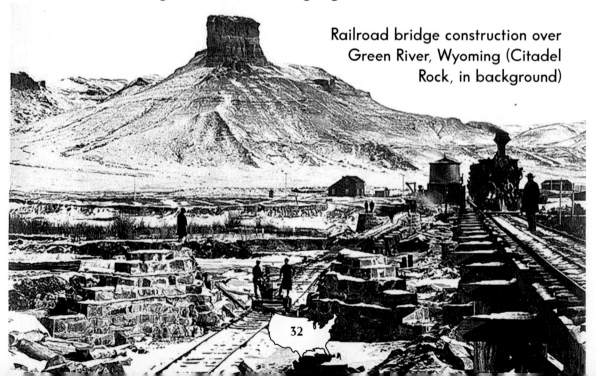

Railroad bridge construction over Green River, Wyoming (Citadel Rock, in background)

On March 4, 1869, General Ulysses Grant became president of the United States. Four days later, the Union Pacific arrived in Ogden, Utah. Approaching from the West, the Central Pacific was only 50 miles (80.5 km) away, and still no meeting place had been chosen. President Grant ordered Grenville Dodge to bring the parties together and settle the question. Dodge and Collis Huntington met all night and, being more practical than their bosses, came to an agreement. In the morning, Dodge informed Congress that the railroads would join their tracks at **Promontory Summit** on the north shore of the Great Salt Lake.

As the railroads neared the joining place, the Central Pacific crew proved what it was made of. Charles Crocker had bet Thomas Durant $10,000 that his crew could lay 10 miles (16.1 km) of track in a single day. Crocker chose April 28 as "Ten-Mile Day." He selected eight strong Irishmen and Chinese, who put everything they had into the task. They began at 7:00 a.m. and at 7:00 p.m., James Strobridge declared victory. The eight men, supported by about 1,000 others, had laid 10 miles and 56 feet (16.11 km) of rail. Each of the eight had lifted 250,000 pounds (113,500 kg) of iron and spiked 3,520 rails (weighing 560 pounds [254 kg] each) to 25,800 railroad ties. As a bonus, Crocker gave each track layer four days' pay. It was never recorded whether Durant paid the bet.

On May 8, 1869, Stanford headed east from Sacramento on a special train. While he was crossing the Sierra, Durant's train, traveling west, was stopped by laborers who had not been paid. They refused to let the train continue until Durant paid them $500,000. He wired for money and an assistant wired for troops, but railroad workers intercepted the messages. They threatened violence and a general strike if troops should arrive. Finally, Durant gave the men $450,000, keeping $50,000, and they released him.

This delay postponed the celebration joining East and West until May 10, 1869. On May 4, a friend of Stanford's, **David Hewes**, had learned that nobody had prepared a special souvenir for the historic event. He quickly had $400

Scene before driving the Last Spike,
Promontory Summit, Utah Territory, 1869

worth of gold made into a 5-5/8 inch (14.4 cm) long golden spike. It was engraved with the words "May God continue the unity of our Country as the Railroad unites the two great Oceans of the world." On top of the spike it said "The Last Spike." This spike became famous as "the Golden Spike." Three others were made and used in the ceremony: a silver spike from Nevada, a gold and silver spike from Arizona, and a smaller gold spike made by a San Francisco newsman.

Illustration of the Golden Spike

The Central Pacific's tie contractor had a beautiful railroad tie carved from California **laurel**. It was inlaid with a silver **plaque** that said "The last tie laid on completion of the Pacific Railroad, May, 1869." Because the gold and silver spikes were too soft to hit with a hammer, four holes were pre-drilled into the tie.

Illustration of the last tie

35

(Far Left) a replica of the Central Pacific's Jupiter and (Left) a replica of the Union Pacific's No. 119

The two mighty locomotives—"Jupiter" from California, and No. 119 from the East—stood facing each other about 58 feet (17.6 m) apart at Promontory Summit. The Union Pacific had built 1,006 miles (1,716 km) of track and the Central Pacific 690 miles (1,110 km) of track. Jupiter burned wood and had a round, funnel-shaped smokestack, while No. 119, a coal-burner, had a narrow, straight stack. All over the country waiting Americans prepared to celebrate the uniting of East and West.

(Below) scene after the joining of the tracks at Promontory Summit, Utah, 1869. Jupiter is parked on the left and No. 119 on the right.

POEM:
WHAT THE ENGINES SAID

What was it the Engines said,
Pilots touching—head to head
Facing on a single track,
Half a world behind each back?

....

....

Said the Union: "Don't reflect, or
I'll run over some Director."
Said the Central: "I'm Pacific;
But when riled, I'm quite terrific.
Yet today we shall not quarrel,
Just to show these folks this moral,
How two Engines—in their vision
Once have met without collision."

That is what the Engines said,
Unreported and unread;
Spoken slightly through the nose,
With a whistle at the close.
- *by Bret Harte*

Workers put the special tie in place and laid the last rail sections across it. Leland Stanford carefully pounded the two golden spikes into two holes. Then Thomas Durant placed the Nevada and Arizona spikes into the remaining holes. Stanford and Dodge gave short speeches. Workers replaced the precious metal spikes with iron spikes. Both Stanford and Durant swung at one of the iron spikes with a sledgehammer and missed! One iron spike had been specially wired to a telegraph line so that the sound of the blows could be heard across the country. A railroad worker hammered the spikes into the tie, and Western Union telegraphed the long-awaited message at 12:47 p.m.— D-O-N-E.

A telegraph pole sticks out above a railroad track. It was used to relay messages across the country.

WHERE THE SPIKES AND TIE ARE TODAY

The Golden Spike and silver-plated hammer are in Stanford University Museum in Palo Alto, California. Arizona's spike is at the New York Metropolitan Museum. The laurel tie was in the California Pacific's San Francisco office when it burned to the ground in the earthquake and fire of 1906. On July 30, 1965, the Golden Spike National Historic Site was created near Promontory Summit. Two replicas of the locomotives "Jupiter" and "119" can be seen there, along with replicas of the historic spikes and hammer, and the ceremonial tie. The National Park Service holds reenactments of the Golden Spike Ceremony on May 10 every year.

Close-up view of the replica of the Union Pacific's No. 119

Church bells rang out across the nation, and even the **Liberty Bell** in Philadelphia was rung again. Cannons were fired in San Francisco, New York, and Washington, D.C. All across America, people set off fireworks and held parades. Seven thousand people packed the Mormon Tabernacle in Salt Lake City. At Promontory Summit, the locomotives were disconnected and moved forward slowly until they touched. Their engineers blew the whistles, and everyone cheered as workers smashed champagne bottles against the engines. Jupiter was backed up and No. 119 came forward until it sat where Jupiter had sat. Then the process was reversed so that each train sat for a moment over the junction of the two lines.

Stanford held a festive luncheon in his personal railroad car. He and Durant made speeches and sent telegrams to national leaders and other **dignitaries**. The festivities of the day ended, but the national transformation that it marked had just begun. Within a week, people were riding trains from New York to San Francisco in only seven days! A journey that had once cost $1,000 by wagon now cost from $70 to $150. Mail and freight rates fell drastically as well.

In 1893, crippled by Durant's mismanagement, the Union Pacific went broke. It was reorganized under new owners and still exists today. The Big Four worked hard to maintain the Central Pacific's **monopoly** in the West. When investors tried to form the Southern Pacific Railroad in 1864, which would connect San Diego with San Francisco and Missouri, the Big Four quickly bought out the line. By the 1880s, the Big Four's transportation network was securely in place, though in 1884 the Central Pacific was renamed the Southern Pacific. In a 1901 novel, *The Octopus*, **Frank Norris** described the monopoly that Stanford and his partners had achieved. He compared the snorting locomotive to "…a vast power, huge, terrible, flinging the echo of its thunder over the reaches of the valley, leaving blood and destruction in its path…the iron-hearted Power, the monster, the Colossus, the Octopus."

A broadside advertising trains heading west

In spite of the corruption and scandals that accompanied the transcontinental railroad, it transformed America. It immediately linked western mines with eastern markets. The nation's economy was no longer at the mercy of ocean storms, which had sunk many ships, including some carrying gold. Building and running the railroads created a huge demand for timber and coal. Between the 1870s and 1900, railroads consumed more than 20 percent of the nation's cut timber. Iron and steel production multiplied 10 times between 1864 and 1900. Oil, discovered in Pennsylvania in 1859, caused a rush similar to the California Gold Rush. Between 1864 and 1900, oil production increased twenty-fold.

Within a few decades, the United States became the world's economic leader. Its internal market was the largest on earth, and that market was now within reach of every American. Crop growers could concentrate on whatever grew best

Citadel Rock, Green River Valley, by William Henry Jackson, photographer for U.S. Geological Survey of the Territories, 1870s

because regions no longer had to be self-sufficient. By 1900, manufacturing output had passed that of Britain, Germany, and France combined. Although the population had doubled between 1870 and 1900—partly because new jobs brought millions of immigrants—the United States was able to feed, clothe, and house its citizens better than ever before.

KEY PEOPLE IN THE HISTORY OF
THE TRANSCONTINENTAL RAILROAD

Allen, Horatio (1802-1899) - American civil engineer and inventor.

Casement, Dan (1832-1881) - Shared construction supervision responsibility of the Union Pacific line with his brother, Jack.

Casement, John ("Jack") (1829-1909) - A construction supervisor of the Union Pacific line. Went on to build other railroads across the country.

Crocker, Charles (1822-1888) - American merchant and railroad builder.

Dodge, Grenville (1831-1916) - Civil war general and chief engineer of the Union Pacific Railroad construction.

Douglas, Stephen A. (1813-1861) - American political leader; senator from 1847 to 1861.

Durant, Thomas (1820-1885) - A founder of the Union Pacific Railroad; a financier and capitalist.

Hewes, David - San Francisco contractor and supplier to the Central Pacific Railroad.

Hopkins, Mark (1814-1878) - American merchant and railroad builder.

Huntington, Collis (1821-1900) - Hardware merchant and railroad builder.

Jefferson, Thomas (1743-1826) - Third president of the United States (1801-1809).

Judah, Theodore (1826-1863) - American civil engineer and railroad surveyor.

Lincoln, Abraham (1809-1865) - The 16th president of the United States (1861-1865).

Norris, Frank (1870-1902) - San Francisco writer, author of *The Octopus* (1901).

Sherman, William (1820-1891) - Brigadier general of volunteers during the Civil War; took over command of the Army from General Ulysses Grant in 1869.

Stanford, Leland (1824-1893) - American railroad builder and politician; founder of the Central Pacific Railroad and of Stanford University in Palo Alto, California.

Stevens, John (1749-1838) - New York inventor and engineer who built the first operating locomotive in the United States.

Strobridge, James H. (1827-1921) - Miner and railroad builder from Vermont, took charge of the Central Pacific's construction in 1864.

Whitney, Asa - (1797-1872) American inventor and manufacturer of railroad cars and machinery.

A Timeline of the History of
— The Transcontinental Railroad —

1826	First American railroad (horse-drawn) opens in Massachusetts.
1829	Horatio Allen brings an Iron Horse from England and tests it at a Pennsylvania coal mine.
1840	There are 3,000 miles (4,800 km) of railroad lines in the East.
1853	Congress authorizes a survey of the proposed Pacific Railroad. Results published in 1855.
1859	Abraham Lincoln and Grenville Dodge discuss the best route for a Pacific Railroad.
1860	Theodore Judah surveys the Sierra Nevada for a crossing point.
6/28/1861	Judah and the Big Four incorporate the Central Pacific Railroad of California.
1861-1865	The American Civil War.
1862	Congress passes and President Abraham Lincoln signs the Pacific Railroad Act. It names two companies and directs them to build a transcontinental railroad.
10/26/1863	The Central Pacific begins construction east from Sacramento, California.
11/2/1863	Theodore Judah dies from yellow fever.
12/1/1863	The Union Pacific breaks ground at Omaha, Nebraska, but lack of funding delays construction.
1864-1868	The Southern Pacific Railroad is formed and the Central Pacific acquires it to stamp out competition.

1865	The Union Pacific lays its first track from Omaha. The Central Pacific solves its manpower shortage by hiring Chinese construction workers.
1866	The Casement brothers and Grenville Dodge take charge of Union Pacific crews. Congress authorizes the Central Pacific to proceed beyond the California/Nevada border.
1867	The Central Pacific finishes the summit tunnel and crosses the crest of the Sierra Nevada Mountains. The Union Pacific crosses the Rockies.
1867	The Pullman (sleeper) car, refrigerator car, and air brake are invented.
1867-1868	Attacks on the railroad by Sioux, Cheyenne, and other Plains tribes bring about their removal to reservations.
5/10/1869	A ceremony marks the driving of the final spikes of the transcontinental railroad at Promontory Summit, Utah.
1871-1889	Chartered in 1864, the Northern Pacific Railroad breaks ground and is built between Olympia, Washington, and western Montana.
1872	The Union Pacific's Credit Mobilier scandal emerges.
1885	The Central Pacific name disappears as the company merges into the Southern Pacific.
1893	The Union Pacific goes bankrupt and is reorganized.
1901	Frank Norris publishes his novel, *The Octopus*.
1938	Railroad service to Promontory Summit is discontinued.
1965	The Golden Spike National Historic Site is created near Promontory Summit.

GLOSSARY

alternate - Arranged first on one side, then on the other, at different points along a line.

assets - The entire property of a person or corporation after payment of debts.

black powder - An explosive mixture of potassium (or sodium) nitrate, charcoal, and sulphur.

bond - A paper representing money owed; a piece of paper sold to raise money that will be paid back in the future with dividends.

brakeman - A train crew member who inspects the train and helps the conductor.

capitalist - A person who invests money in business; a believer in the economic system that features private ownership of wealth.

convention - An assembly of persons meeting for a common purpose.

Corps of Topographical Engineers - An entity created by the War Department in 1813 to survey and map for military purposes; in 1863, merged with the Army Corps of Engineers.

dignitary - A person of high rank.

Donner Summit - A pass over the Sierra Nevada Mountains made famous by the party of 87 emigrants led by George and Jacob Donner in 1846. Only 47 of them survived the winter.

financier - A person who deals with finance and investment on a large scale.

flatcar - A railroad freight car with no permanent raised sides, ends, or covering.

frontier - A border between two countries; a region that is on the margin of developed territory.

grade - Ground level; degree of inclination of a slope or road.

groundbreaking - Event or ceremony associated with the first shovel of earth overturned for a construction project.

historian - A student or writer of history.

incorporate - To form into a legal entity called a corporation.

interest - A charge for borrowed money, usually a percentage of the amount borrowed.

Iron Horse - Nickname for a locomotive, especially a steam locomotive.

laurel - A family of evergreen trees, also called "bay tree."

Liberty Bell - Historic American bell dating from 1753, which was rung in July 1776, marking the signing of the Declaration of Independence.

lobby - To try to influence public officials, especially members of government.

logistics - The handling of the details of an operation.

monopoly - Exclusive ownership, possession, or control.

motive - Something that causes a person to act.

nitroglycerin - A heavy, oily, explosive liquid used in making dynamite.

nomadic - Roaming about from place to place, without a fixed home.

parallel - When referring to latitude, a line running east-west around the globe and measured from the equator to describe a location on the Earth.

Pawnee - A Native American people originally from present-day Kansas or Nebraska.

pilot - A wedge-shaped device mounted at the front of a locomotive to push away obstacles from the track that could derail the train; also called a "cowcatcher."

plaque - A flat, thin piece, often of metal, used for decoration.

Promontory Summit - A place 32 miles (51.5 km) west of Brigham City, Utah, on the north end of the Great Salt Lake, where the Central Pacific Railroad and Union Pacific Railroad joined tracks in May 1869.

Republican - U.S. political party founded in 1854.

right-of-way - The strip of land over which a public road or railroad is built, and over which the road or railroad has first rights.

secede - To withdraw from an organization or nation.

share - Any of the equal portions into which property or invested capital is divided.

Sierra Nevada - Spanish for "snowy saw-toothed mountains"; a high mountain system in eastern California.

sledgehammer - A large, heavy hammer swung with both hands.

subsidy - A grant by a government, person, or company to help with a project considered to be for the public good.

summit - The highest point; peak.

Summit Tunnel - The tunnel the Central Pacific dug at the Donner Pass before heading downhill into Nevada; it was 1,659 feet (505.7 m) long and took two years to build. It is now bypassed by the railroad and sits unused.

terminus - The final goal; end of the line.

territory - A geographical area; in the United States, an area under its control, with a separate legislature, but not yet a state.

topographer - Mapmaker.

transcontinental - Extending across a continent, such as a railway.

yellow fever - An infectious, often fatal disease of warm regions, which is carried by a particular mosquito.

Books of Interest

Crewe, Sabrina and Michael V. Uschan. *The Transcontinental Railroad (Events That Shaped America)*, Gareth Stevens, 2004.

Evans, Clark J. *The Central Pacific Railroad*, Children's Press, 2003.

Halpern, Monica. *Railroad Fever: Building the Transcontinental Railroad 1830-1870*, National Geographic, 2004.

Isaacs, Sally Senzell. *The First Railroads (The American Adventure)*, Heinemann Library, 2004.

Magram, Hannah Strauss. *Railroads of the West*, Mason Crest Publishers, 2002.

Weitzman, David. *The John Bull: A British Locomotive Comes to America*, Farrar, Straus & Giroux, 2004.

Web Sites

http://www.pbs.org/wgbh/amex/tcrr/index.html

http://inventors.about.com/library/inventors/blrailroad.htm

http://www.uprr.com/aboutup/history/

http://cprr.org/Museum/index.html

http://www.sphts.org/

INDEX

Linda Thompson is a Montana native and a graduate of the University of Washington. She was a teacher, writer, and editor in the San Francisco Bay Area for 30 years and now lives in Taos, New Mexico. She can be contacted through her web site,

http://www.highmesaproductions.com